SOUL TRAIN

Books by Allison Joseph

What Keeps Us Here (1992)
Soul Train (1997)

SOUL TRAIN

POEMS BY

ALLISON JOSEPH

CARNEGIE MELLON UNIVERSITY PRESS
PITTSBURGH 1997

ACKNOWLEDGMENTS

The author wishes to thank the journals where the following poems first appeared:

Nebraska Review: "Home Girl Dreams A Dance Partner"
Callaloo: "In the Bookstore"
Spoon River Quarterly: "Adolescence"
Eyeball: "Soul Train"
Pittsburgh Quarterly: "Persuasion", "Exhibitionism"
Pacific Coast Review: "The Effort of Travel"
Unsettling America: Race and Ethnicity in Contemporary American Poetry: "Junior High Dance"
Calliope: "Dance Fever"
Muleteeth: "Young Marrieds"
Agni Review: "The Inner Life", "Good Humor" (later reprinted in *On the Verge: Emerging Poets and Artists)*
Orange Coast Review: "Home Girl Talks Girlhood"
Green Mountains Review: "Home Girl Steps Out"
Blunt Object: "Nightclubbing"
The Wedding Anthology: "Wedding Party"
Cimarron Review: "Used Books"
Half Tones to Jubilee: "Immigrants", "Anatomy"
Poet and Critic: "Livelihood"
Crazyhorse: "Genealogy"

I wish to thank the Illinois Arts Council for a literary fellowship which aided during the writing of these poems. Also thanks to the following individuals whose friendship has been invaluable: Rodney Jones, Martha Christina, Carolyn Alessio, Gretchen Knapp and Maura Stanton.

The publication of this book is supported by a grant from the Pennsylvania Council on the Arts.

Library of Congress Catalog Card Number: 96-83423
ISBN 0-88748-247-3
Copyright ©1997 by Allison Joseph
Printed and bound in the United States of America

10 9 8 7 6 5 4 3 2 1

TABLE OF CONTENTS

I

II

III

IV

I

Good Humor

In our neighborhood of run-down houses,
of abandoned lots and corner groceries,
nothing tasted better than ice cream's

sweet delight: the delicate peaks
and swirls of vanilla soft-serve,
cold chill of Italian ices

scraped from their containers
with tiny wooden spoons—cherry
and rainbow staining teeth, gums.

How we loved orange push-ups
that melted down our fingers,
so sticky we couldn't help

licking our thumbs and fingertips,
palms grasping at the slippery
treats. Remember the red, white

and blue bomb pops, sugar
and color frozen on a stick,
popsicles almost too heavy

to handle, almost too large
for the child-mouths that
welcomed them, sucking until

the colors faded, until
pallid ice was left behind.
All the flavors we could want

lived in the white truck
that cruised our streets
on summer afternoons: coconut

and chocolate, strawberry shortcake
and lemon-lime, peach and succulent
pineapple pulling us through
those heavily humid summer days.
We'd listen for the faint music
of that truck, wrangle dollars

and quarters from parents,
grandparents, and line up,
one behind the other, ready

to cool our tongues, freeze our teeth,
longing to lick and swallow everything
that melted beneath the summer sun.

SOUL TRAIN

Oh how I wanted to be a dancer
those Saturday mornings in the
living room, neglecting chores

to gape at the whirling people
on our television: the shapely
and self-knowing brownskinned

women who dared stare straight
at the camera, the men strong,
athletically gifted as they

leaped, landed in full splits.
No black people I knew lived
like this—dressed in sequins,

make-up, men's hair slicked
back like 40's gangsters,
women in skin-tight, merciless

spandex, daring heels higher
than I could imagine walking in,
much less dancing. And that

dancing!—full of sex, swagger,
life—a communal rite where
everyone arched, swayed, shimmered

and shimmied, hands overhead
in celebration, bodies moving
to their own influences, lithe

under music pumping from studio
speakers, beneath the neon letters
that spelled out SOUL TRAIN—

the hippest trip in America.
I'd try to dance, to keep up,
moving like the figures on

the screen, hoping the rhythm
could hit me in that same
hard way, that same mission

of shake and groove, leaving
my dust rag behind, ignoring
the furniture and the polish

to step and turn as they did,
my approximation nowhere near
as clever or seductive, faking

it as best I knew how, shaking
my 12 year old self as if something
deep depended upon the right move,

the righteous step, the insistent
groove I followed, yearning to get
it right, to move like those dancers—

blessed by funk, touched with rhythm,
confident in their motions, clothes,
their spinning and experienced bodies.

BIG SHOTS

for April

Not much violence when you lived
in the Castle Hill projects, just
broken elevators, odors of piss

rising from graffiti-sprayed stairs.
You lived at 525 Havemeyer, apartment
7E, middle daughter of three,

your mother separated or divorced,
I never knew which. Your best friend
at 13, I was skinny to your fat,

our minds formless, full of tv,
pop songs we'd sing out loud
on the way home from school:

What's the matter with the clothes
I'm wearing—don't you know that
they're outta style? We could dance

like rock stars, grabbing
imaginary mics to sing into,
forgetting that your eyes didn't

quite move together, that I
was too thin, clothes ill-fitting.
We'd get good grades, but didn't

hesitate to laugh at our teachers,
mocking the loud ties our principal
wore, scoffing at his plaid jackets,

polyester pants. We owned
Henry Hudson Junior High, smart-ass
kids who stepped through the halls,

hands over our mouths hiding smirks,
teasing our scraggly math teacher
until we hoped we tried his patience,

making fun of his long hair, beard,
the rips in his rough jeans.
That was our first try at bravado,

the first time lust made us lie,
telling each other no woman could want
his lanky form, hippie clothes.

But who wanted us? We didn't know,
weren't slick enough to be sure
anyone ever would, our bodies

learning to quicken at something
other than the songs on the radio,
better than the silly Bee Gees.

Like Billy Joel sang, *it's still
rock-n-roll to me*—and I still
hum songs aloud, voice not as strong

as ours together were on the way home
as we chattered about Mr. Drillings—
his clumsy ways—scrawling numbers,

dropping chalk—the gray streaks
in his thick tousle
of shoulder-length hair.

We walked and sang with energy
we couldn't contain, belting
words we didn't understand

or bother to comprehend, hoping
the lyrics could carry us far
past our bodies, into confidence.

JUNIOR HIGH DANCE

No one wanted to dance with us
in 8th grade, to glide across
the shiny expanse of gym floor,
choosing us from among
the awkward and shy girls,
the boys loud and pushing instead,
uncouth to everyone but chaperones.
I had on the ugliest pantsuit—
matching orange and blue—
homemade by my mother before
before she dazzled us with
cotton and corduroy.
My best friend had an earache,
but stayed anyway, swaying
to the music, letting it
carry her heavy body
a little forward, away
from the wall, back.
The speakers didn't wail
the way I wanted them to,
their volume respectable,
although you could hear
Diana Ross singing—*I'm coming out*—
her anthem of disco liberation.
We watched the other kids dance,
lithe Hispanic girls who always
seemed to know when to turn,
how to bow and shimmy, or smile.
Watched the older black girls
who, self-satisfied and worldly wise,
knew all the latest steps,
and the variations on the latest
steps, so when I dared once before
to venture on the dance floor,
they hooted at me, said *that's old*,
with surety they had about nothing

else. April and I hung back,
sassy wallflowers joking about
our teachers—their whiteness,
their lack of street savvy.
They still thought Diana Ross
was a Supreme, that she still sang
You Can't Hurry Love with Flo and Mary,
that Motown was still Hitsville, USA.
No one could convince us
we had something to learn
from them, no one could tell us
they were anything more than old
as they blew up balloons,
made sure the lights stayed on.
And we had our corner,
our tiny bit of that place,
where we listened to that garish
dance music, not letting
our bodies stray far, staying
right there, no matter how funky
the beat, no matter how delicious.

ADOLESCENCE

No one calls you beautiful
at 14, or knows the longings
that fill your body, except
the other girls who lurk late
with you, the awkward emerging
women you are becoming
fragile as the puff
you powder yourselves with,
the mirrored compact.
Too early to love
any man, though you're learning
the trappings: leather heels,
lipstick, tight hose dark
around legs that tremble
beneath cold street lights.
Too early for breasts,
for the full flesh that marks
your passage from one another
into the arms of lovers.
In clear night air,
all you have is the silence
of waiting together,
of learning the rules
of attraction: the walk,
the talk, the hair,
the perfume you spray
on each wrist,
behind each ear,
along the vulnerable throat.

FACTS OF LIFE

Hiding the book in my hands,
I'm hesitant, unsure—gawky
at thirteen as I thumb its pages

secretly, discreetly, glancing
at its contents, peeking,
longing to know, yet afraid

to know, sweat beading
on my palms, neck, the
small of my back. Finding

this manual in a corner
of the library, tucked
away as if no one ever

wanted to know the body's
recesses and paths, its
channels of pleasure, I

open to charts—diagrams
of the male body—sneak
looks at meek line drawings,

vague terrors taking me as I
stare at inexact sketches,
at words I don't dare speak.

I don't know the male body's
skin or sweat, ignorant
of textures, sensations,

but I want to, curious for
something beyond pictures,
needing to discover. How shamed

I'd be if a boy caught me here,
immersed in this book despite
myself, despite trying to pull

from its technical words:
erogenous zones, arousal,
contraceptive, orgasm.

Unsure what all this means,
uncertain of what my body's
learning, feeling,

I'm embarrassed by its growth:
timid breasts tender beneath
my shirt, body all angles.

Years would pass before I'd
let myself look at a man—
at thighs and skin, soft hair

above the penis, slow moves
unfolding before my eyes,
motions no pictures could match,

movements no diagrams could predict,
my hands hesitant still, shy but
able to reach, touch; willing

to seek like I did that day
in the library—eyes gliding over
those male and female anatomies,

figures that gave no clues
to sex's tensions, its great
shudders, fevers.

Home Girl Talks Girlhood

Remember that longing for hips
and breasts, the rising curves
of womanhood? Honey, I was

so skilled at wishing
for a body I didn't know
what the hell to do with:

round, proud, everything
high and firm, long legs
curved just so, a dancer's

bearing. Just who I was
going to lure with all this,
I didn't know—all I did know

was that I quaked, afraid
each time I had to pass
those boys on the corner,

their eyes inspecting me,
finding what wasn't there,
calling after me—*you ugly,*

too skinny, for real.
How much time did I waste
longing to be a woman,

fooling around in Mother's
make-up—slashes of red vivid
against my lips, loose powder

freed on her dresser top.
I'd forage among bottles
of perfume, spray myself

with musk's dark odor,
fingers stained by mascara,
rouge. And when she'd find

me, she'd demand *just what
you think you doing, you
no damn woman yet,* and I'd

wait again, hoping my body
would begin, hoping to be
like her—all business,

all woman as she wiped
the paint from my face,
smoothing on cream to clean

my skin, bringing me back
to my ashy girlhood self,
muted child of color.

II

To the Lost Daughters of Bronx Science

Where are you now, Carol Aronowitz,
sassiest Jewish girl I ever knew,
with your red-gold hair and your dreams
of Greenwich Village nightclubs,
your poems which begat my poems,
your small shoulders that did not sag,
your anger, your fire, your strut
that cheered me out of gym class
into the school parking lot where
I nearly keeled over, clutching
my stomach as menstrual cramps rolled
through it? And where are you now,
Georgiana Hsu, with your courtesan's
smile and easy grace, your round
seductive Asian face troubled
by mathematics, your romances
found in dime-store paperbacks
that you read faster than anyone,
trading them before the school day
began, before chemistry and physics
left us all baffled, a little less wild?
Where are you, Smita and Cathy,
sisters by choice—one of you dark,
Indian, the other pale, Irish,
both of you crazy enough to insist
on being friends in a world that
divides by color, brave enough
to take on Manhattan, dressed
for dancing at the Peppermint Lounge
or Underground, underage girls
needing a fix of nightlife, assurance
of a world beyond chem lab, history class,
beyond the PSAT, SAT, those scores
that finally tested nothing but patience.
And where is Karen Chin,
who showed me the proper way

to use chopsticks, and Claudia Probst,
who believed the power of words
went way beyond our leaden textbooks,
and Edna Bondoc, and Someng Tsang,
and Cyrilline Crichlow, too—
where is she—all those girls who knew
how to move through this world, who
knew that city like a gift, turning
it inside out, using it, walking
its streets, taking subways, buses,
wise in the ways of mass transit.
And where is Afrodesia McCannon,
who first showed me the sooty aisles
of the Strand Book Store, who got
chased out of a Chinese restaurant
with me, our tips too meager?
And what of Berni, Cathy, and Gail,
black girls who dared venture
into Lord and Taylor's, aware
that the woman following us
was a security guard, making sure
we didn't steal what we couldn't buy.

They're gone now,
first to Yale, Cornell, Oberlin,
Barnard, Princeton, Wesleyan,
and then beyond, hurtling headlong
into marriages and jobs, still
smarter than their teachers,
into law school and graduate school,
still smarter than their professors,
into lives I've lost track of,
their dazzling projects lost to me,
new feats I know nothing of but can
imagine, girls who chose me as friend,
who didn't overlook or underestimate me,
who taught me a multiplicity of customs,
mannerisms, colors, bits of different

languages from all across the city.
For four years in that squat Bronx
building, you taught me to gossip,
to dance, to lose myself in sudden
hysterical teen-age laughter over
boys or evil teachers, our futures
hovering, though safely out-of-reach,
beyond us in moments of comradeship,
confidences shared in bathrooms or
across crowded lunchroom tables,
secrets I no longer remember anything of
except how close they brought us,
such friendships bountiful, sustaining,
far more real than tests or grade point
averages, far keener than what
I know now, lulled by adulthood.

IN THE BOOKSTORE

Here I find refuge, though the woman
behind the counter looks at me

as if I can't read, regarding me
as just another colored girl

who might steal her store
out from under her, who might

rip pages from paperbacks,
ruin hardcovers with rough

handling. But her suspicion
can't stop me, however she looks

at me she won't stir from
her chair, afraid as I'm afraid,

both of us moving but not
moving, me shuffling

through tight aisles,
her pencil tapping, tapping.

She waits for me to figure out
whatever it is I want,

will be glad to silently ring up
my sale, hand me my small sack.

But I'm intent on lingering,
shifting my weight from one foot

to another, taking book after book
in my hands, holding each one

a long moment before I replace it,
before I hand her the one I'll take

back with me to the Bronx,
where rumor has it no one reads

unless it's the *New York Post's*
daunting, garish headlines.

I'm 21, with twenty dollars and two
subway tokens in my pocket, greedy

for the life of the mind,
that energy, needing it enough

so when this woman hands me my change
I hiss a whispered *thank you*,

make sure my eyes catch hers
for one second of indictment,

one moment where I'm right, she's wrong,
and there are still dollars in my palm.

HOME GIRL STEPS OUT

Tonight I look so good,
so long and lean with ambition,
I startle myself with beauty.
Sure, I could let myself
grow lonely in my living room,
consoled by talk shows, news,
soaps set in towns so white
snow covers the ground all year.
But tonight, I'm stepping out,
freeing the self that's longed
for some groove, beat, or rhythm,
carrying myself as proudly
as Aretha, Gladys, or Patti,
a sister unafraid to glitter
these long nights, sashaying
through smoky clubs to sway
on the floor, hips in motion,
shoulders moving, my beauty
evident as I hum to the music,
catching the beat, the drum,
the steady pulse beneath it all.
Girlfriends say, *Damn, you look good,*
and I do, better than a college
education, better than a winning
lottery ticket. I'm ticking
myself, heels clicking on tile,
fingers snapping, and I'm
daring any man worth his name
to come on and join me,
twirl under the smoke
and heat, whispering my name
during pauses in the music,
gliding with me ever so slowly
and softly during slow songs,
the low-lights, do-it-to-me
ballads. But if no one appears,

if no man is real enough
to dance with the woman
in the slick leather skirt
and red pumps, I'll still
keep stepping, lights playing
off my white silk shirt,
head aloft. Moment by moment,
I'll learn myself, the woman I am,
set loose, apart, free.

TEN YEARS LATER

the pain's here still, though not
as dense as it was at 15, familiar now
as the skin of my back, my body.

Back then, I curled in fear,
hidden in a bathroom stall,
the blood always a surprise,

my cycle not yet fact in my mind,
foreign as the full breasts I saw
on older girls, as the hair

now downy at my groin. No one
said it would be all right,
these changes necessary, good,

the pain normal, natural
as the bright spot reddening
my panties. Ten years ago,

I cursed my awkward elbows,
skinny legs, fearing
I wasn't feminine except

for the secret rush of blood
each month, the cramps that
stopped me with their aches.

I thought it cruel to call
me female, looked nothing
like women on tv—no curves, confidence,

no clothes to make seduction real.
How natural it seemed to them—
the legs, make-up, and hair,

their lips and hands ready
for possibilities I could
imagine, not know. Ten years

later, my body's my own,
I've banished shame to embrace
hips and thighs, breasts fuller,

a woman now in place
of a girl, every month's blood
signaling all's right, body

coming full circle again,
my cycle no longer laden
with fear, no longer an

aberration I could not speak of.
Each month, I recall that girl
driven by fear to dwell

in a bathroom stall, how she
feared what her body was
letting go, how wounded, unsure.

Now, this flow opens me to life,
pain informing me I'm alive
among all the worldly changes.

HOME GIRL DREAMS A DANCE PARTNER

Let me tell you, finding that ideal man
isn't easy, you could search the dance halls

and nightclubs from here to Kingston
and still not find that one man

who moves graceful and easy, his feet not timid,
his arms flowing instead of jerking.

I don't care if the music's calypso,
fast-dub reggae or rock-your-body house,

New Jack Swing or slow grind,
he's got to have the moves to stop

all the others in their tracks, stunning
high and mighty women, their haughty fellows.

When that man takes the floor with me,
he'd better know how to glisten and smile,

no bowed-head shuffling or meek, reluctant
steps. He'd better know how to glide,

how to move his hips from side to side
so that everyone watches, jealous of me,

my tremendous good fortune. I'm asking
for someone confident, not cocky,

someone self-assured, not arrogant,
someone who knows the music not as

casual friend, not as acquaintance,
but as lover, unafraid to move

in a way that's almost feline,
feminine, blurring the line

between my sex and his, our bodies
together, arms round each other

as the dance-hall crowd gathers about,
busy with talk, admiration

for a couple riding a delicate rhythm
nothing can break as we move from

song to song, tempos changing quick.
I could search from here to Montego Bay,

crash rent parties in Brooklyn or
Port-au-Prince, and still not find

the one man willing to step out
in his finest tailored clothes,

a suit that would no longer look good
after an hour of serious dancing.

Even if I never find him, I am not
content to sit home, music within

too strong for a night of television
in a dark room. I am going out

to throw up my hands and dance
the jubilation anyway, because

a woman never knows who will step up,
offer a cool drink in a long glass.

III

"DANCE FEVER"

There's that couple again,
spinning beneath the massive
disco ball, competing for cash
and prizes worth more than

they'd ever seen, more than
they'd ever know. That couple,
of course, is us, an unlikely
pair moving under hot lights,

dancing toward the edge
of the stage and back,
hoping there's no
trap door, no sudden drop

from the disco pop and
sizzle. Tonight, I'm
the girl in trouble,
the one you might like better

if you slept with her,
face void, tamed under
make-up for a studio
audience. I'm spandex,

sparkle, a flash of leg
beneath a neon pink skirt,
silver lamé top, a hustler,
a freak, an endless vibe

that knows how to smile
for the camera, faking
the pleasures of nightlife.
But no matter how I try,

our dance is always off-beat,
and you're moving away from me,
through the 70's, 80's, and 90's,
leaving behind this bad girl,
this Donna Summer devotee
who could never master the art
of slow dance, shy glide.
You're moving to your own

rhythm, to the whine of wheels
inside your head that won't
stop for anyone, a shuffling
two-step you learned

in dancing school, bad luck
streak intact. And when our
minutes on the floor are up,
we'll pace small rooms

of our own, cloisters
where there's only
skin on skin, try
for the passion music

can't provide, can only
hint at, our fever subsiding
to a pulse, a good beat
that's easy to dance to.

YOUNG MARRIEDS

Always inhabiting someone else's lives,
transients without homes or rooms,

we dwell a month here, stay one
there, our belongings packed,

stored away from reach, our lives
full of the temporary's lore:

coarse rustle of moving boxes,
ragged suitcases piled high

in a friend's damp basement.
Used to building lives

only to take them apart,
we tread gently into friends'

and relatives' houses, trying
not to harm dishes, keepsakes,

intent on not wearing out
any welcome. Grateful,

we use what is left us:
a bed in which we sleep,

turn, and love, kitchen
where we fumble with knobs

and unknown switches,
bathroom where we find

ourselves, bodies nude
beneath shower spray,

your hands rubbing soap
on my belly as if to hint

at something there, a future
of permanence and peace,

our lives rooted in place,
no longer notorious.

PERSUASION

Who needs your hands
more than I, woman
who's crossed miles
to be with you again?
Surely you can think of no one
who's made her need more plain:
red dresses, loose pants,
blowzy gauze shirts
you can see right through,
skin blushing ready.
I miss your placid fingers
on the buttons of each blouse,
want you to flick me loose
from clothes, revealing
my body's broad work,
smooth, uncharted places.
I've wanted to touch you,
to woo you hour upon
hour, kissing the fine skin
over your temples, the timid
path from throat to abdomen.
Tonight, if you're willing,
we'll abandon all those
tepid signs of romance:
roses, wine, that creepy
heart-shaped box of candy.
We'll turn and stir instead,
ready for quick strokes,
sudden moves, fingers
finding the easy places,
corners where lust
makes itself known,
where need waits
to be spent—nerves
crouched in wait, senses
poised at pleasure's edge.

Ready to give in, we'll
let the night close in
around us, shutting out
everything but our two
human forms, our grip
on each other growing
tighter, impossible to deny.

EXHIBITIONISM

Risqué means risk, uncovering
what normally stays covered,

letting the world in on
all my body's secrets:

the scar that runs like a slit
down the back of my calf,

the shape of the nipples
that top my breasts,

the breasts themselves—
round, lush, not sculpted

or muscular. It's all
on display—long legs,

ample hips, bare back
seldom seen in sunlight.

But this is no magazine,
no 25 cent Times Square

peep show too passé
to watch again, no trick

pen where the lovely model
disrobes before your eyes.

I'm human, a woman
circa 1995, fragile

as anything, durable
as anything, naïve

but world-wise, still
hushed by first touches,

by skin on skin.
This is the woman

who rises slowly each
morning, standing

before mirrors to bathe
herself, water rushing

into the sink, washcloth
rough against her skin

as she wakes completely,
lather warm on her belly.

This is not a model
or mannequin,

no dime-store pin up
or locker room centerfold.

At risk of losing you,
I'm admitting imperfections,

letting you see flesh, hear
my voice, observe my stride

as I keep my motions going,
moving as intuition dictates—

back and forth before you,
in and out of your vision.

Soul Suite

By day, this apartment
looks like any other:
books and unkempt clothes

in disarray, newspapers
piled by the back door.
But when night falls

and I'm all alone,
this place transforms
to my soul suite,

a spotlight dance
with no audience.
Here I can improvise,

make it all up from
nowhere—gliding,
stepping, marching

to music as if
I'd never heard it
before. No one cares

if I'm wickedly
clumsy, or slow
and uncertain;

no one watches
to see if my balance
is off, body heavy.

No applause
if I'm subtle,
graceful, no one

to impress, and I'm
not trying. I only
want to keep it

moving, one foot
in front of the other,
hips shaking from

side to side, arms
overhead, then down.
When I'm moving

I don't have to speak,
and no language
can tell my story

anyway—no words
can move me like
a strong single note

sung over piano
riffs, no phrases
rival bass kicking

in, drums taking
over. Naked,
naïve, true

to patterns
of bob and weave,
spin and turn,

I'm making moves
far into night,
unaccompanied

by anyone else,
grateful for
solitude, for

those instinctive
moments of bend
and reach, stretch

and slide. How else
would I learn
to throw arms

wide, how else
could I come
to this oasis:

dark room empty
of its daily shapes,
freed by nightfall.

MORNING KISS

I come to you with the scent of apple
on my fingertips, grazing your hair,
your chest, your eyelids that flutter

and blink from sudden light.
I come to you honest, smelling
like work or love, like good exercise,

no excuses shaming my body, no
alibis. I no longer need to lie,
to hide from male eyes,

because your eyes do not probe
or scar, your mouth not turning
to a signal of scorn. Instead,

you let me touch its damp corners,
my fingers gliding across their sheen,
or you smooth your lips across

my back, onto the trembling nape
of my neck. You inhabit me
without possession, not holding

me back or down, so when
I come to touch you there's
no fear, nothing scared caught

in my throat. There's sweetness instead:
apple on my fingers, taste of fruit
on my lips; my mouth awaiting yours—

joining with you this morning
as we do each morning—humbled, revealed,
but knowing the heat of one persistent kiss.

Solace

in a world where spirit
is denied, your hands
matter, loving as they skim

my skin, trace bruises
or scars, the room dim
around us, quiet in calm.

You soothe my surfaces,
follow paths with your
fingers, knowing

the grain, texture,
delivering your blessing
deliberately, stroke

upon delicate stroke,
motion you can not
and do not stop, until

I am dizzy from your
touches, reeling
from bold contact—

such sensuousness.
Your hands encompass
opposites: softness

of belly, dampness
of hair, slickness
between breasts,

shoulder blades.
As your hands
bring me closer

and again closer,
I shut my eyes,
let go of facts,

figures; letting
my body buck,
move, heave,

and finally sigh,
loosened from all
but gravity, freed

as if forgiven, stirred
by your swift hands,
shaken by solace.

The Inner Life

Today I dare to claim the unnamed,
the deep febrile inner life

I slough off each month, loss that's
one less life gravitated to earth,

no matching sets of x and y,
chromosomes not to build their life

in me, not yet. I'm not yet sad
for that loss, feel no remorse

to wash your seed from me, rinsing
away its scent, the heat I've come

to love, your signature inside me
trailing off to disuse. So much

of what we have we don't use,
content to let our bodies go

only so far before we pull back, out,
stopping to watch each other, take

each other in. Yes, I'm muscle, sinew,
cartilage, artery—yes, my body is gaining

and losing, just as yours is gaining
and losing, our potential seemingly

infinite, as we could not wear away,
never leave behind bones becalmed

and drained. This is chemistry:
this mixing and turning, diminution

of cells and waste, a lessening
I know each month as damp, secret.

Not out of shame now, but out of awe,
I carry this secret, feel allegiance

to the jazzy mechanics of birth, its names—
Fallopian tubes, ovum, uterus.

I can hum these names to myself,
steady against the pain, cramps

pulling deep strings within
the belly. I can chant

this inner life, feel its tension
and release, constriction and ease.

And I can give that life to you,
knowing it safe from ridicule,

knowing it can grow one day
into inestimable riches, wealth of birth.

NIGHTCLUBBING

We dance where souls are chic,
dramatic in their moves, sleek

and untamed, where bodies mingle
under tense strobes emitting

bands of multicolored light
that leave surfaces glinting—

the mirror behind the bar,
the long rows of shiny bottles

filled with clear or amber
liquids. I spin on that

dance floor, dress unspooling
behind me, a flag of surrender

unfurling, a signal that I'm
giving in to the pulse of this

music, percussion from speakers
moving me past this moment,

past all the moments that threaten
to hold us back, keep us down.

Here we're vulnerable, elemental,
music luring us to reveal

what we usually hide: arms,
shoulders, legs, midriffs bare.

Partner in this dance, you move
closer, then away, finding me

among fellow dancers,
committing dark, sultry moves

that won't soon be forgotten—
gliding, crouching, weaving

your body like it was meant
for nothing but this ritual

of man and woman, ceremony
performed among others too busy

to notice. They're lost in steps,
in arching and bending

that takes them further into
this realm where lights caress

each face, where we look
more beautiful than we ever

thought we could, no cover
on grace, on motions

that don't cease after last call,
after all club doors close.

WEDDING PARTY

I wanted to have a wedding
where a band called Sexual Chocolate
would play cover versions
of "Turn the Beat Around"
and "Got To Be Real", tunes
so disco everyone's forsaken them
in the oh-so-cynical '90's.
I wanted my bridesmaids
in orange tulle, groomsmen
in light green, their cummerbunds
so wide their waists became
some thick, enticing region,
regal as an alleyway.
I wanted folks to glide
onto the dance floor,
doing quaint, antiquated dances
like the funky chicken, Latin hustle,
polyester divas doing moves so fine
even Shaft himself would have
to stop, grin his approval.
I wanted finger foods
in snack sizes, a wedding cake
piled so high in gumdrops
and coconut that no one's
blood sugar level would be safe.
I wanted it crass, and big,
and ugly, bad enough
to make relatives shudder
whenever they remembered
my denim patchwork gown,
platform heels. Instead,
I'm here at the city clerk's office,
an ordinary woman in an
ordinary dress, marrying
an ordinary man in ordinary
shoes. Still, I know that party

is going on somewhere, if only
in the strange regions of my mind:
music and costumes
by Earth, Wind, and Fire,
catering by Momma and Company,
and the m.c., of course,
is a dapper black man
who wishes us *love, peace, and soul,*
our lives one everlasting ride
on the Soul Train bound
for Boogie Wonderland,
li'l Stevie's harmonica
blowin' us one last tune
in the key of life.

IV

SLOW JAMS

Tonight I'm just another listener
to late-night radio soul, hearing
song after song of longing,

singing along with the choruses,
the female back-up singers
featured on almost every song

to give counterpoint to male
desires, echoing words like
kiss or *eyes* or *baby*, a

vocabulary of want they voice
again and again. Tonight
I want pure, unabashed

emotion, tight streetcorner
harmonies, love-man raps
spoken lusty and slow,

high notes soaring
from the world's best divas—
Chaka Khan, Gladys Knight,

and the jammin' Teena Marie,
funkiest white girl on the planet.
No limits to love when I

listen to these songs, nothing
held back in the delivery
of this break-up-make-up

music, the d.j.'s declarations
spinning out over the airwaves:
Roger and Cassandra, Kim

and Andre, Leslie and Darnell
forever. Nowhere else is need
so obvious, ardently revealed

in titles like *Slow Motion,*
Honey Love, Quiet Storm.
Tonight I'm listening to fill

hours without you, moments
I can't reach for my man.
Loving long-distance,

I send it far beyond
this radio station's range,
past miles that mark

hours between us. Only
music this rich could span
those lengths, full

as symphonies, sonatas.
So I'm not ashamed to sing
my own shaky harmony

with ballad after ballad,
unafraid to linger on long notes
with lights low, radio on.

USED BOOKS

Their dust clogs nostrils,
soils hands—a fine
ancient silt heady as ash;

weak spines letting loose
pages delicate as old mail,
dulled by humidity, sun.

Buying used books
is dangerous business,
trust that something

remains when you pry them
from shelves, covers torn.
When you buy a copy

of *Sonnets From the Portuguese*,
you know you've bought
someone else's timid gift,

an offering not meant
to be resold, but here
it is, perched between

Elements of Chemistry
and Dante. A Hallmark edition,
you sense it was given

out of someone's shy passion,
heartsick longing not unlike
the Brownings', but groping,

inarticulate, nervous enough
to buy a gift shop's book
of sonnets, soothed by that

perfect ornamental form.
Now this cardboard edition's
romance is reduced for resale,

its cover blanched like a sick
girl or pale suitor distracted
by love, its pages wan as lace.

You open the slim volume
to let its poems breathe,
to permit *isolate pure spirits*

a place to stand and love in
for a day, lingering over
language too rarefied

for these dusty shelves,
too rare in these days
where all that is new breeds.

THE EFFORT OF TRAVEL: BRONX, NEW YORK

Worn, weather-beaten,
this city doesn't age

gracefully, instead
bulges and creaks

in use, blunt
and broad, serviceable,

prodigal streets cracking
under mass transit,

heavy rush hour traffic.
From the bus window,

I view it intimately,
a frequent rider averting

my eyes from the people
who travel with me:

tired mothers with babies,
old men with racing forms

folded back, Catholic schoolers
in sturdy shoes and uniforms,

public schoolkids who jostle
and fight, cursing aloud.

I have trained myself
to look out the window,

to study this mutable
landscape of bars and stores—

for rent signs, fire sales,
going-out-of-business racks

of clothes hanging limply
out front, picked over

too often to look new.
It would be too easy

to call this stubborn,
mottled place beautiful,

to admire its scuffs
of graffiti, leaving it

at some comforting literary
adjective, forgetting

the effort of travel—
the shock of tires over potholes,

the weary arms of the driver
as he pulls around corners,

the thin hands of a girl
clutching a metal handle

overhead, fingers taut
as we pass red brick homes

with faded awnings, lots
of weed-grasses and rocks,

ugly public schools the bus
pulls up at, letting off

kids swinging unwieldy texts
scribbled in arithmetic,

scratchings of previous students
unerased, indelible

as street signs.
It would be too easy,

so I stay wary, watchful,
vigilant as the peddlers

who inhabit these corners,
shouting their bargains aloud.

New York Scenes

I: Barter

Small shops throb
in the shadows of the rickety el,
radios tuned to the loud, fast pulse
of disco, the beat-laden horns
of salsa, as Saturday crowds
bargain hunt overstocks:
cheap clothes from Korea
or Taiwan, junk jewelry,
hand towels, bars of soap—
discount merchandise I can't
resist touching, taught never
to buy new, to wait
for the slashes
on the price tag,
brash marks of savings.
I fondle dollar-a-pair
gilt earrings, jewelry boxes
painted a rich wood hue,
lined in the fake silk
girls covet. I learned
to shop here as a girl,
to search each rack
for the right size,
right color, my hands
passing over the stained
or ill-fitting, examining
goods for flaws the eye
can easily excuse.

II: Chinese Kitchens

Almost every neighborhood, you can find them,
bare storefronts in yellow and red,
their menus, in Spanish and English, taped

to the front window, bulletproof glass
keeping customers from the kitchen
where fried rice makes a skittery music
in the woks, the air fragrant, oily.
In places like this, you get nothing fancy—
scanty versions of dishes sold for more
in sit-down restaurants, this menu
strictly take-out, served with plastic
packets of dark soy, chow mein noodles
in wax paper bags, white rice that cools
to blocks of starch. I come here for
fast, cheap food, knowing no one
will ask me anything but my order,
the impersonal personal as the slithery
lo mein noodles I come here craving,
loving their salty length. I don't care
that the food, second-rate, leaks grease
through the carry-out boxes, or that
the woman behind the glass must ask twice
what I want, translating my request
to a language the cooks know, urgency
of hot oil against metal in her voice
as she yells from cash register to kitchen.

III: En Route

Late night, Castle Hill glows with neon,
the avenue's signs lit past closing time.

I have stood here countless times,
waiting for a bus while gypsy cabs

cruised the avenue, blasting
car radios, blaring horns

to lure in their fares.
This late at night, it's foolish

to wait for a bus, to covet
the cold metal token in my palm.

But how I know this place: corner bar
where men crouch round an aged tv.,

movie theater turned bingo hall
I swear I've never seen anyone enter,

candy store where the front window
never changes—unclaimed toys, sooty

practical joke kits. And how this
city glows when I'm alone—

things bitter and shopworn
look promising again beneath

intermittent light of streetlamps,
somehow valuable. En route,

I'm passing through again,
the journey warm with such

comforts, waiting while the cabs
speed with their needed grace,

hustling for another
night's worth of fares.

LIVELIHOOD

Mother worked in hard-luck places,
neglected brick buildings perched
on the outskirts of the city,
perilous as old mansions.

Hardly aware of her world
of pay stubs and bills,
I shied from the children
she nursed, a child myself,

fearing eyes that did not focus,
noises of pain and hunger
that rose insistent, unmitigated,
a howling I heard nowhere else.

She fought to keep them clean,
wiped feces and urine from
their bodies, her eye clinical,
always looking for cuts or sores,

soothing on ointment with cotton
swabs, touching blue-black flesh
gingerly, wiping sleep from
the corners of their eyes.

She'd pace long gray halls
holding hands with a shy girl,
a blushing child with Downs' Syndrome,
or calm an angry, stuttering boy,

making what she could of
guttural speech, his arms
and hands flailing, fitful.
At home, at dinner, I heard

her say unfamiliar words:
mongoloid, thorazine, laceration.
Laughing, she'd tell stories—
which client had been bad
or greedy, whose relatives
had dared visit the musty halls,
the damp cavernous rooms
and tiled corridors,

the other home she knew
and negotiated so surely,
far from my prying eyes,
my timid terrors.

IMMIGRANTS

for my parents

In our small hot kitchen
my parents cooked cho-cho
and callaloo, breadfruit

and the beautiful conch,
the lambi my father loved,
stewing it for hours

at a time, some part
of his island coming back
for him, his tongue.

Coconut milk, coconut water,
cloves and allspice,
ginger, curry, nutmeg—

all made that house
aromatic, made them forget
the mortgage of America,

the yoke of bills, companies.
Oh the taste of dasheen,
of saffron and mace,

all the spices of Jamaica
and Grenada transplanted
here, just as my parents

were transplanted, their
accents strange in this
nation that did not treasure

what they did: pigeon peas
and plantains, saltfish
and sugarcane, the sweet

sweet flesh of the tender
mango—yellow pulp easy
on the tongue, gracious

in the mouth, welcome
as any island song,
any calypso remembered

by daughters turned too American,
sons who know nothing of cassava
or guava, as any memory of home.

TRANSIT

for my mother

You never learned to take
the wheel beneath your palms,
to drive down our rocky

driveway, bags packed,
heart finally emptied.
You knew how to take it,

how to stand just enough
of my father's demands,
listening warily to diatribes,

explanations: *A black man*
cannot make it in this
country. No diatribes though

for you, no solace
for your place in history.
You'd sit, shoulders

hunched while you sewed,
brown hands busy threading
needles, tending the finest

cloth you could afford,
the heaviest wool, feeling
its nubby texture.

You knew its weight
would warm you through winter
into spring, during days

of travel on drafty buses,
cold subways. I have spent
those hours too, riding miles

on trains, face close to glass,
wondered how it felt for you
to leave every day with your

heavy purse, nurses' shoes,
skirt of plain gray wool.
You didn't know how to walk

away from anything, to drive
off in exhaust and dust.
Moving steadily, slowly,

you knew you'd arrive
where you needed to be,
despite derailments, breakdowns,

despite hours of waiting
for the train to come,
to lift you far above

the city, to cradle you
down below, taking you in
its silver body, moving

you through tunnels,
stations, destinations,
tiled halls and corridors.

ANATOMY

How does it feel for him
to study the body again,
reciting facts, names,
places where the body

gives way, gives up:
aorta, arteries, veins,
thin threadlike capillaries,
grasping four-chambered heart

separated into left
and right, atrium and ventricle.
Late at night he studies,
spends hours over pages

of anatomy and chemistry,
his eyesight dimming,
vision tired from tiny
printed text, diagrams

and charts, plots
of the human body,
long names of disease:
diabetes mellitus, carcinoma,

leukemia, arteriosclerosis.
Does he know his own body
any better, my father studying
at fifty, understand the mishaps,

the chronic disorders
of metabolism that force him
to stick himself each day—
needle into arm, insulin

injected with a twinge
he's grown used to,
a grimace appearing
on his face, arms

sore from years of pricks.
Does he understand my mother's
body, lungs that fight to fill,
her chest cavity blemished

with cancerous spots,
her breathing labored,
inhalation and exhalation
more effort now than

ever, her speaking voice
hushed by disease,
made raspy and low
by something she can't

control, a phenomenon
he studies as night
turns into morning,
learning terms for

her pain: neoplasm,
malignant, biopsy, radiation—
words he whispers until
his time is up, the test before him

with its blanks and spaces,
choices of a, b, or c;
its terse and necessary questions
asking only for the facts.

GENEALOGY

I

Dim dance hall light.
  Fragile pleats end
just above my mother's

thin, brown ankles,
  red carnations bloom
at her waist.

Leaning against a wall,
  hands thrust behind,
she's restless, rustling

in blue, shirred silk.
  In this damp room,
she's cold—miserly

central heating hardly
  rising beneath her dress.
Outside, the British chill

bows asters to earth,
  spiked stars, bent stalks.
Head down, she sways

as couples shuffle past,
  moving to the insistent music,
keeping time with her body.

Precarious on points
  of high heels, lovely
and awkward, she'll lean until

that man with the single scar
   sidles up, sharp pleats
on baggy trousers,

spit-shined shoes. They
   will take turns at shyness,
flushed with this night,

until she takes his hand,
   moving, beginning
the dance, rhythm of cha-cha

and merengue driving
   them forward
into the music's reckless

percussion, its promise,
   its pulse spinning
my parents, not letting go.

II A Photo

They stand together, touching
   along lengths of arms,
and I can't tell if they hold
   hands, or merely let bodies
touch. Her arms are long,
   too long for the sweater
she wears; it hunches under
   her armpits, leaves wrists
and forearms bare. Stooping,
   head and shoulders hunched,
she's not taller than my father,
   who buttons only one button
on his jacket, deliberately
   casual, a small smile lifting
his cheeks into roundness.
   She's in pleats from waist

to calves, smiling face lit
in happiness. 50's black
and white, their faces almost
colorless, brown faded gray.
They lean on a fence in a country
I have never seen, newlyweds
on holiday, brazen in their travel,
their pleasure, their foreheads
smooth, unwrinkled, eyes squinting
into the glaring sun.

III

For an instant, in the mirror,
I swear I saw it—my mother's body

instead of my own—pocked flesh,
puckered navel, stretched skin

of knees and elbows, aged chips
of toenails. Squatting naked

in our blue bathtub, she slung
a ragged, soapy washcloth

onto thighs, hips, chest,
hoarding the water as if

still a Jamaican schoolgirl,
the tub only half-full.

When she turned her back to me,
I knew to lean down over her,

to cup my hands in the water,
pouring it over back and shoulders,

rinsing where she could not reach.
Her back would glisten with it,

scars gleam as if they had never hurt.

IV

Clutter of change and pencil stubs,
keys for locks that no longer work,
one burnt-out television set.

I find myself among the unwieldy
stuff of my father's life—

lottery tickets and parking fines,
smooth white mounds of bills.
This room is full of things

love can't repair, remnants
of homes in other countries,

this house the last in our
chain of immigrant stops—
London, Toronto, New York,

last home for any of this.
My mother's sewing machine

sits untouched in the corner.
I tried once to set it whirring,
but my fingers caught between

needle and presser foot, cloth
snagged, seams crooked

as my father's sly bets.

V

Today a restive urge to clean
 has me on my knees,
picking lint off the carpet,
 fingers like my mother's,
long, fine. I clean the table,
 long wipes of a rag,
remember her swift hands
 on its surface.
In the linen closet, clothes
 were stuffed low,
no longer smelling of her,
 and I knew again
the hoax of the body,
 the regeneration
that did not come—
 my father and I
in a hospice room high
 above the city,
cleaner than the streets,
 the stubby grasses below.
Her body seemed all bone,
 skin stretched to cover,
thinned past adolescence,
 childhood, chemo scars
ridged into her arms.
 In that clean room,
I surrendered, knew only
 the few words she
had left. Now I kneel
 in our house, body
rocking with stories,
 all I inherited
staring back at me,
 waiting for touch.

1982
The Granary, Kim R. Stafford
Calling the Dead, C.G. Hanzlicek
Dreams Before Sleep, T. Alan Broughton
Sorting It Out, Anne S. Perlman
Love Is Not a Consolation; It Is a Light, Primus St. John

1983
The Going Under of the Evening Land, Mekeel McBride
Museum, Rita Dove
Air and Salt, Eve Shelnutt
Nightseasons, Peter Cooley

1984
Falling from Stardom, Jonathan Holden
Miracle Mile, Ed Ochester
Girlfriends and Wives, Robert Wallace
Earthly Purposes, Jay Meek
Not Dancing, Stephen Dunn
The Man in the Middle, Gregory Djanikian
A Heart Out of This World, David James
All You Have in Common, Dara Wier

1985
Smoke from the Fires, Michael Dennis Browne
Full of Lust and Good Usage, Stephen Dunn (2nd edition)
Far and Away, Mark Jarman
Anniversary of the Air, Michael Waters
To the House Ghost, Paula Rankin
Midwinter Transport, Anne Bromley

1986
Seals in the Inner Harbor, Brendan Galvin
Thomas and Beulah, Rita Dove
Further Adventures With You, C.D. Wright
Fifteen to Infinity, Ruth Fainlight
False Statements, Jim Hall
When There Are No Secrets, C.G. Hanzlicek

1987
Some Gangster Pain, Gillian Conoley
Other Children, Lawrence Raab
Internal Geography, Richard Harteis
The Van Gogh Notebook, Peter Cooley
A Circus of Needs, Stephen Dunn (2nd edition)
Ruined Cities, Vern Rutsala
Places and Stories, Kim R. Stafford

1988
Preparing to Be Happy, T. Alan Broughton
Red Letter Days, Mekeel McBride
The Abandoned Country, Thomas Rabbitt
The Book of Knowledge, Dara Wier
Changing the Name to Ochester, Ed Ochester
Weaving the Sheets, Judith Root

1989
Recital in a Private Home, Eve Shelnutt
A Walled Garden, Michael Cuddihy
The Age of Krypton, Carol J. Pierman
Land That Wasn't Ours, David Keller
Stations, Jay Meek
The Common Summer: New and Selected Poems, Robert Wallace
The Burden Lifters, Michael Waters
Falling Deeply into America, Gregory Djanikian
Entry in an Unknown Hand, Franz Wright

1990
Why the River Disappears, Marcia Southwick
Staying Up For Love, Leslie Adrienne Miller
Dreamer, Primus St. John

1991
Permanent Change, John Skoyles
Clackamas, Gary Gildner
Tall Stranger, Gillian Conoley
The Gathering of My Name, Cornelius Eady
A Dog in the Lifeboat, Joyce Peseroff
Raised Underground, Renate Wood
Divorce: A Romance, Paula Rankin

1992
Modern Ocean, James Harms
The Astonished Hours, Peter Cooley
You Won't Remember This, Michael Dennis Browne
Twenty Colors, Elizabeth Kirschner
First A Long Hesitation, Eve Shelnutt
Bountiful, Michael Waters
Blue for the Plough, Dara Wier
All That Heat in a Cold Sky, Elizabeth Libbey

1993
Trumpeter, Jeannine Savard
Cuba, Ricardo Pau-Llosa
The Night World and the Word Night, Franz Wright
The Book of Complaints, Richard Katrovas

1994
If Winter Come: Collected Poems, 1967–1992, Alvin Aubert
Of Desire and Disorder, Wayne Dodd
Ungodliness, Leslie Adrienne Miller
Rain, Henry Carlile
Windows, Jay Meek
A Handful of Bees, Dzvinia Orlowsky

1995
Germany, Caroline Finkelstein
Housekeeping in a Dream, Laura Kasischke
About Distance, Gregory Djanikian
Wind of the White Dresses, Mekeel McBride
Above the Tree Line, Kathy Mangan
In the Country of Elegies, T. Alan Broughton
Scenes from the Light Years, Anne C. Bromley
Quartet, Angela Ball
Rorschach Test, Franz Wright

1996
Back Roads, Patricia Henley
Dyer's Thistle, Peter Balakian
Beckon, Gillian Conoley
The Parable of Fire, James Reiss
Cold Pluto, Mary Ruefle
Orders of Affection, Arthur Smith
Colander, Michael McFee

1997
Growing Darkness, Growing Light, Jean Valentine
Selected Poems, 1965-1995, Michael Dennis Browne
Your Rightful Childhood: New and Selected Poems, Paula Rankin
Headlands: New and Selected Poems, Jay Meek
Soul Train, Allison Joseph
The Autobiography of a Jukebox, Cornelius Eady
The Patience of the Cloud Photographer, Elizabeth Holmes
Madly in Love, Aliki Barnstone